The Colony of New Hampshire

Susan Whitehurst

The Rosen Publishing Group's

PowerKids Press™

New York

For Joyce Whitehurst

Published in 2000 by The Rosen Publishing Group, Inc.
29 East 21st Street, New York, NY 10010

Photo Credits: p. 1 © 1999 North Wind Pictures; pp. 4, 7, 11, 15 © The Granger Collection; p. 8 © Bibliotheque Nationale, Paris/Lauros-Giraudon, Paris/Superstock; p. 12 © 1998 North Wind Pictures; pp. 16, 20 Superstock; p. 18 © 1994 North Wind Pictures; p. 22 © 1997 North Wind Pictures.

First Edition

Book Design: Andrea Levy

Whitehurst, Susan
     New Hampshire / by Susan Whitehurst.
          p.   cm. — (The library of the thirteen colonies and the Lost Colony series)
     Includes index.
     Summary: Provides an introduction to life in the colony of New Hampshire, from its founding to the American Revolution.
     ISBN 0-8239-5477-3
     1. New Hampshire—History—Colonial period, ca. 1600–1775—Juvenile literature. [1. New Hampshire—History—Colonial period, ca. 1600–1775.]
     I. Title. II. Series.
     F37.W49 1999   98-32367
     974.2'02—dc21   CIP
                                                                                                 AC

Manufactured in the United States of America

Contents

Hereditary Country
of the
Iroquois

Crown Point

Ticonderoga

Ft George

Ft Miller
Ft Hardy

Saratoga

ALBANY

Kinderhook

Kaskill
Point

Livingstone

CHAMPLAIN

LAKE CHAMPLAIN

LAKE GEORGE

N E W

Y O R K

C O U N T Y

A L B A N Y

Mohawk R

C O U N T Y

V E R M O N T

G L O U C E S T E R C O U N T Y

Norwich

Ware

Windlor

Weathersfield

Rockingham
Nº2

N O C O U N T Y

C U M B E R L A N D C O U N T Y

Connecticut R

Nº4
Nº4
Nº3
Nº5
Nº2
Nº8
Nº7
Nº6
Nº5
Nº9
Nº8
Nº Almsbury

Nº1

Nº2

PROVINCE LANDS

Concord

Canada

Canada

Westermost
Township

Newfram
Ington

Nº3
Boston

Deerfield

H A M P S H I R E

Old Rutland

KUSUMPE
POND

WINIPISIOKET
or POND

SQUAM
POND

Gillmans
Town

Bowlers Grant
Town

P R O V I N C E   O F

N E W

H A M P S H I R E

PROVINCE
LANDS

Chester Brent
ford

Kingstown

Southampton

Derwick

York R

C. Nidduk R

Durham

Merrimac R

Hampton R

E A S T E R N P A R T O F M A S S A C H U S E T S

C O U N T Y O F

Y O R K

Sawakotuk or Sawko R

New
Marble
Head

Boston

Gorham
Town

Cape Elizabeth

Wood Islands

Sawco Bay

C. Porpus

WELLS
BAY

Isles of Shoals

B A Y

P R O V I N C E   O F

M A S S A C H U S E T S   B A Y

H A M P S H I R E

W O R C E S T E R

Gore

Oxford

Groton

M I D D L E S E X

ESSEX

Andover

Cape Ann

Marblehead

Chelsea

BOSTON

Nahant Pt
Pull Bay
The Graves

Kanokessil Rocks

North R

Walpole

Halifax

Hanton

SUFFOLK

Gurnet Point

MASSACHUSETS

B A Y

Cape Codd

C A P E   C O D   B A Y

BOWLES'
NEW ONE-SHEET M
OF
NEW ENGLA
comprehending the Provin
MASSACHUSETS
AND
NEW HAMPSHIR
with the Colonies of
CONNECTICUT & RHODE I
DIVIDED into their COUNT
Townships, &c
Together with an Accurate Pl
the Town, Harbour and Envi
of BOSTON.

Printed for the Proprietors BOWLES &
Nº 69 in St Pauls Church Yar
LONDON.

Explorers in the New World

Hundreds of years ago people from all over the world came to America to find a new life. They settled in **colonies** that became the United States. In the 1600s, several **explorers** came to the land that would later be known as New Hampshire. Martin Pring came to this area in 1603. He was looking for a shortcut across America to Asia. He also hoped to find **sassafras** trees. The bark from this tree was used to make sassafras tea, a popular drink. Although Martin Pring came to the area first, it was Captain John Smith who officially **claimed** New Hampshire for England. John Smith had founded the colony of Virginia in 1609. Five years later, he explored the area Martin Pring had visited, made maps, and claimed the land for England.

◀ *John Smith claimed the land that would later become New Hampshire.*

5

New Hampshire's Early Settlers

In 1622, King James of England gave the land Smith had claimed to John Mason and Sir Ferdinando Gorges. Mason lived in Hampshire, England, so he named the new land New Hampshire. In 1623, David Thomson and 20 Englishmen built New Hampshire's first settlement, Pannaway Plantation. In 1629, Mason and Gorges divided up their land. Gorges took the area that would become Maine. Mason took New Hampshire. Although John Mason never came to America himself, he sent **settlers**. In 1630, they built their town near a field of wild strawberries. They called it Strawberry Bank.

Pannaway Plantation is now the town of Rye. Another settlement, built in 1623, was called the Dover settlement. It is still called Dover today, although now it is a modern town.

King James was head of both the church and the government in England. ▶

6

Algonquian Indians

Settlers in New Hampshire soon met the **Algonquian** Indians, who had been living in the area for hundreds of years. The Algonquians lived in villages of 50 to 200 people. They were very **resourceful**. When the Algonquians killed an animal, they used all the parts. They ate the meat and made clothes and **moccasins** from the skin. They used bones for needles.

Chief Passaconaway, whose name meant "child of the bear," was a wise Algonquian leader. He saw that it would be useless to fight the settlers and told his people not to make war. The Indians introduced the settlers to food like **succotash** and popcorn. In the winter, they taught the settlers to make snowshoes with branches and strips of leather. They also taught them to pack meat in snow to preserve it.

Algonquian Indians belonged to many different tribes, but they all spoke the Algonquian language.

9

Making a Living

Almost everybody in New Hampshire grew their own food. The land was covered with trees and rocks. Before the farmers could plant, they had to chop down the trees and move the rocks. The farmers used the rocks to make rock walls around their fields. Many of those rock, or stone, walls are still standing in New Hampshire today.

Settlers grew corn, beans, and pumpkins. They raised sheep, cows, chickens, and pigs. New Hampshire settlers also made money fishing and hunting. They shipped millions of pounds of fish to Europe every year. They also sent beaver furs to Europe. The furs were made into hats and coats.

Today, New Hampshire is nicknamed "the Granite State" because of all the granite rock in the land. It is also said that "the people are as tough as granite," meaning they are proud and strong.

Codfish fishing was one way that New Hampshire colonists made a living. ▶

Lumber

New Hampshire had so many trees that colonists could make a living building ships. They also sent lumber to Europe. The great forests in England were almost gone, but New Hampshire was filled with trees. The best trees were the white pines. They were straight and tall. Some white pines were as much as 200 feet tall. The English Navy wanted the white pines to make **masts** for their ships.

The "mast pines" were marked and sent to England. A colonist could be arrested if he cut down one of the King's pine trees.

◀ *Cutting down a large pine tree took many men to do the job.*

Meeting Houses and Schools

Each New Hampshire town built a meeting house. The meeting house was used for all-day church services on Sunday. It was also where the men decided how the town should be run. Town meetings still take place in New Hampshire today.

In 1641, Massachusetts **annexed** New Hampshire. England turned New Hampshire into a Royal colony in 1679, which separated it from Massachusetts again. While New Hampshire was still part of Massachusetts, a school law was passed. The law said that towns with 50 families or more should have a school and a teacher. It also said that everybody in the town, not just families with children, should help pay for the school. Money was scarce, so the teacher was often paid in corn. This is how our modern-day public school system started.

Schoolhouses were usually just one room. Children of all different ages learned together. ▶

The French and Indian Wars

While the colonists were farming, fishing, and sending the children to school, the English and the French were fighting over the colonies. Each group wanted to rule the land, and both wanted the Indians to fight on their side.

The Indians could see that the English had come to stay and that the more towns the English built, the more land the Indians lost. Most of the French had come to hunt and trade, not to build towns that took away land from the Indians. Because of this, the Indians sided with the French. The fighting was called The French and Indian Wars. It lasted 74 years and thousands of colonists and Indians were killed. In the end the English won and stayed, the French lost and went home, and the Indians had to move farther and farther into the **wilderness**.

◀ *These wars were not between the French and the Indians, they were between the French and the English. The English named the wars for the people they fought.*

Talk of Revolution

The King of England thought the colonists should help pay for The French and Indian Wars so he told the colonists they had to pay more **taxes**. New Hampshire colonists were already upset that the King was taking all of New Hampshire's best trees to build ships. New taxes on tea and newspapers made them even more upset. Some colonists refused to pay the taxes. England sent soliders, called Redcoats, to make the colonists pay taxes. In 1774, leaders from all the colonies met in Philadelphia for two months to figure out what should be done. These **Colonial** leaders talked about a revolution, or fighting for their independence from England.

The colonists drank a lot of tea until the British began to tax it. The colonists started drinking coffee instead. They also made a new kind of tea from local sassafras trees. They called it "Liberty Tea" because they drank it instead of tea that came from England.

Fighting broke out after the British sent the Redcoats to the colonies. ▶

New Hampshire Takes a Stand

To fight a war against England, the colonists needed **gunpowder**. England had stopped sending gunpowder to America, but there was an English fort in New Castle that had plenty. In December 1774, 400 New Hampshire colonists **surrounded** Fort William and Mary and captured hundreds of barrels of gunpowder.

When the **Revolutionary War** began in April 1775, New Hampshire sent weapons and 5,000 men to help. Warships were built in Portsmouth, and 3,000 men sailed from this **seaport** to attack English ships. Captain John Paul Jones is called the Father of the American Navy. In 1777, his ship, the Ranger, was the first to fly the American flag. Jones often won battles against larger English ships.

◄ *Captain John Paul Jones captured the first British naval ship to surrender to the Americans.*

21

New Hampshire Today

It's no surprise that New Hampshire's motto is Live Free or Die. The people of New Hampshire are proud of their history of freedom.

In the White Mountains is New Hampshire's most famous landmark. The "Old Man of the Mountains" is a granite rock shaped like a man's face. He's watched New Hampshire grow from Indian villages to Colonial towns to the great state it is today.

Robert Frost, whose home in Derry, New Hampshire, is shown above, was a famous American poet. In some of his poems, he wrote about New Hampshire. He wrote about stone walls that have stood through time as symbols of New Hampshire's strength.

1603
Martin Pring came to New Hampshire to look for the sassafras tree.

Captain John Smith claimed New Hampshire for England.
1614

1622
King James gave land in America to John Mason and Sir Ferdinando Gorges.

John Mason sends settlers to New Hampshire.
1630

1776
New Hampshire signs the Declaration of Independence on July 4.

New Hampshire becomes the ninth state.
1788

Glossary

Algonquian (al-GAHN-kwee-in) A group of Indian tribes that lived in North America.

annex (uh-NEKS) When people of one place take over another place.

claim (KLAYM) To take something and say that it belongs to the person who took it.

Colonial (kuh-LOH-nee-ul) Having to do with the period of time when the United States was made up of thirteen colonies ruled by England.

colony (KAH-luh-nee) An area in a new country where a large group of people move, who are still ruled by the leaders and laws of their old country.

explorer (ik-SPLOR-ur) A person who travels to different places to learn more about them.

gunpowder (GUN-pow-dur) A black powder that explodes in a gun and moves the bullet.

mast (MAST) A tall pole that holds up the sail of a ship.

moccasins (MAH-kuh-sinz) Indian shoes made of leather, and often decorated with beads.

resourceful (rih-SORS-ful) Good at thinking of ways to do things.

Revolutionary War (REH-vuh-LOO-shun-ayr-ee WOR) The war Americans fought to win independence from England.

sassafras (SAH-suh-frass) Tree bark used to make tea.

seaport (SEE-port) A place where boats can dock.

settlers (SET-lurz) People who move to a new land to live.

succotash (SUH-kuh-tash) A stew made of beans and corn.

surround (suh-ROUND) To make a circle around.

taxes (TAK-siz) Money that people give the government to help pay for public services.

wilderness (WIL-dur-nis) An area that is wild and has no permanent settlements.

Index

A
Algonquians, 9
annexed, 14

C
claimed, 5
Colonial, 18, 22
colonies, 5, 14

E
explorers, 5

F
French and Indian
    Wars, 17, 18

G
gunpowder, 21
Gorges,
    Ferdinando, 6

J
James, king of
    England, 6
Jones, John Paul, 21

M
Maine, 6
Mason, John, 6
Massachusetts, 14
masts, 13
moccasins, 9

P
Pannaway
    Plantation, 6
Passaconaway,
    Chief, 9
pine trees, 13
Pring, Martin, 5

R
resourceful, 9
Revolutionary War,
    21

S
sassafras, 5
seaports, 21

settle, 5
settlers, 6, 9, 10
Smith, John, 5
Strawberry Bank, 6,
    22
succotash, 9
surround, 21

T
taxes, 18
Thomson, David, 6

Web Sites:

Check out this Web site on Colonial New Hampshire:
http://www.seacoatnh.com/history/colonial/index.html

24